DIVINE ECHOES

72 Hours of Wilderness Whispers in Pursuit of Yahweh

A Transformative Journey of Prayer and Fasting

by E'Von Griffin Jr.

Divine Echoes: 72 Hours of Wilderness Whispers in Pursuit of Yahweh

Published by Ronin XIII Media

Lancaster, Texas

Paperback ISBN: 979-8-9959784-0-4

eBook ISBN: 979-8-9959784-1-1

First Edition, 2026

Trademark application pending: RONIN XIII

TABLE OF CONTENTS

CHAPTER ONE

About the Author

Who Am I

e'Von Griffin Jr. is a passionate man of God committed to helping individuals deepen their relationship with God through the power of prayer, fasting, and physical fitness. A Marine Corps veteran from Dallas, Texas, e'Von is a devoted father to three amazing children, striving to be the greatest example of what a godly man should look like, act like, and love like.

An enthusiastic gym rat, e'Von pushes his physical limits, even during intense 72-hour fasts, relying on the power of the Holy Spirit to sustain him. His desire to serve the kingdom of God motivates him to expand the influence of Yahweh everywhere he goes, in the name of Yeshua.

In Divine Echoes, e'Von invites readers to embark on their spiritual journeys through fasting and prayer, providing space for reflection and personal journaling to enrich their experiences and deepen their connection with God.

My Testimony

As I embarked on my journey of 72-hour autophagy fasting combined with fervent prayer, I never could have imagined the profound impact it would have on my life. In a time of spiritual stagnation and personal struggle, I yearned for something more - a deeper connection with Yahweh and a tangible transformation in my life.

Leading up to this experience, I found myself overwhelmed with the stresses and distractions of daily life. As a Marine Corps veteran and a father, my responsibilities weighed heavily on me. I wanted to set an example for my three children of what a godly man should embody: a protector, provider, peacemaker, and unstoppable superhero.

In this quest for renewal, I committed to a 72-hour fast, focusing on prayer and seeking God's guidance. During those three transformative days, I learned that fasting is not merely about abstaining from food; it becomes a powerful invitation to commune with God.

Throughout this journey, I kept a journal to capture my thoughts, prayers, and revelations. This journal became a sacred space where I could reflect on the whispers of God in the wilderness. In these moments, divine truths were revealed to me, and the burdens I carried began to lift.

The physical changes I experienced reflected the spiritual and mental transformations taking place within me. Most importantly, this fast saved my life; it reignited my passion for prayer, renewed my hope, and solidified my faith in ways I had never experienced before.

This journey became about more than self-discipline; it was about being a faithful servant of the kingdom of God. Allow these pages to guide you toward your divine echoes and wilderness whispers, letting prayer and fasting lead you into a deeper relationship with Yahweh.

CHAPTER TWO

Introduction

Purpose of this Book

Praying and fasting is a transformative practice that unlocks a supernatural connection to the Holy Spirit. This book is designed for men and women of all ages who yearn for a deeper connection with the Holy Spirit. It emphasizes a 72-hour fast with high expectations and maximum intention. Each day features a challenge that must be completed - no exceptions.

For 72 hours, I dare you to give God your full attention. Journal your thoughts, revelations, and experiences. When we seek Him with sincerity, He promises to reveal Himself. Are you ready to embark on this adventure?

Divine Echoes

Journal EVERYTHING! Capture your thoughts throughout the fast, whether through writing, voice notes, or videos. Review these notes after the 72 hours; you'll be amazed at the insights the Holy Spirit imparts.

CHAPTER THREE

Prepare for War!

Spiritual Benefits of Prayer and Fasting

Drawing Closer to God: Fasting creates space for prayer and reflection (James 4:8).

Seeking Guidance: Use this time to seek divine direction (Acts 13:2-3).

Healing Through Faith: Pray for healing (Matthew 9:35).

Repentance and Renewal: Turn from distractions and focus on renewal (Psalm 51:10).

Intercession for Others: Pray for loved ones and their needs.

Strengthening Your Faith: Fasting builds discipline and reliance on God (Matthew 6:25-26).

Special Considerations for Men and Women

Men: The 72-hour fast aligns well with the male biological circadian clock, enhancing spiritual focus and physical endurance.

Women: Acknowledge the impact of hormonal cycles. Avoid fasting during the days leading up to menstruation (at least two days before).

Tips to Avoid Headaches and Discomforts

Gradually taper off caffeine a few days before the fast.

Stay hydrated - drink plenty of water and herbal teas.

Listen to your body and adjust if you experience dizziness.

Prioritize rest leading up to and during the fast.

Incorporate deep breathing and meditation to manage stress.

Pre-game Techniques

2-3 Days Before: Choose your start time, adjust your diet to whole foods, eliminate processed sugars, and increase hydration.

Fasting Guidelines

Drink 2-3 liters of water daily. Add electrolytes - sodium, potassium, magnesium. Engage in meditation and deep breathing to enhance focus.

Breaking the Fast

Start with bone broth or smoothies. Begin with small portions. Gradually incorporate solid foods - boiled eggs, steamed vegetables. Avoid heavy meals in the first 24 hours.

My Charge to YOU!

I know the idea of a 72-hour fast might sound intense, but I believe with every fiber of my being that this journey can bring about some amazing benefits for your health and overall well-being. We are combining the power of fasting with prayer - a chance to forge a bond with your Creator, to seek His guidance, and to find strength in His presence.

Are you ready to step up, to step out, and to embrace this challenge? Let's do this!

CHAPTER FOUR

Wilderness Whispers

Journaling Prompts

1. What do I seek from Yahweh during this fast?

2. How do I feel physically and spiritually as I begin?

3. What revelations arise as I meditate on today's Psalm?

4. In what ways can I apply the lessons from this fast?

5. What commitments am I making to God as I progress?

Why am I Doing this Again?

Scripture Readings

Matthew 6:16-18

Matthew 9:14-17

Zechariah 8:18-19

Isaiah 58:6-14

Joel 2:12-17

Matthew 17:21

Daily Challenge

Cleanse your body and environment. Remove all distractions.

Spiritual Vittles

Breakfast: Psalm 7

Reflect on God's justice and seek His protection.

Lunch: Psalm 13

Cry out to the Lord in times of trouble and trust in His unfailing love.

Dinner: Psalm 23

Embrace the comfort of the Lord as your Shepherd.

What do I seek from Yahweh during this fast?

Continue your reflections...

Continue your reflections...

It's Bigger than Me

Hours 25-48

Scripture Readings

Jeremiah 29:11

Daily Challenge

Speak the name of the Lord out loud before any statement or action.

Spiritual Vittles

Breakfast: Psalm 31

Seek refuge in God and find strength in His mercy.

Lunch: Psalm 33

Rejoice in the greatness of the Lord and His power over creation.

Dinner: Psalm 77

Remember God's mighty works and seek His guidance.

What revelations are arising as you go deeper into the fast?

Continue your reflections...

Continue your reflections...

I am Called to Service

Scripture Readings

Colossians 3:23

Matthew 6:24

Philippians 2:4

Matthew 20:28

Daily Challenge

Share your testimony with five people, praying with them as you part ways.

Spiritual Vittles

Breakfast: Psalm 113

Praise the Lord for His greatness and compassion.

Lunch: Psalm 139

Contemplate God's intimate knowledge of you.

Dinner: Psalm 150

Conclude your fast by praising the Lord.

How has this fast called you to serve?

Continue your reflections...

Continue your reflections...

CHAPTER FIVE

72+

Post-Fast Reflection

Maintain the spiritual momentum and document your insights and the impact of the Holy Spirit during the fast. This experience may be the catalyst to profound healing and transformation in your life.

As you prepare to embark on the journey thereafter, remember: the goal was not just to complete a fast but to deepen your relationship with Yahweh. Through this disciplined approach to prayer and fasting, you can anticipate a revival in your soul.

Now I challenge you to continue to grow and share your experience with anyone who is willing to listen. Lead your own small groups and families in this challenge. Make disciples and keep your sword and armor close.

A Word from E'Von

You made it. Those 72 hours were not easy - they were never meant to be. But you showed up, you pressed through, and Yahweh met you right where you were.

I wrote this book because I needed it first. I was that warrior in the wilderness, exhausted and searching, and it was in the silence of fasting that God's voice became the loudest thing in the room.

Do not let the fire that was lit in these 72 hours burn out. Feed it daily - through scripture, through prayer, through community, and through service. You are not done. This is only the beginning.

Go be the warrior He made you to be. I am proud of you, and more importantly - Yahweh is proud of you.

- E'Von Griffin Jr.

Matthew 28:19-20

Therefore go and make disciples of all nations, baptizing them in the name of the Father and of the Son and of the Holy Spirit, and teaching them to obey everything I have commanded you. And surely I am with you always, to the very end of the age.

Ephesians 6:10-20

Finally, be strong in the Lord and in his mighty power. Put on the full armor of God, so that you can take your stand against the devil's schemes. Take the helmet of salvation and the sword of the Spirit, which is the word of God. And pray in the Spirit on all occasions with all kinds of prayers and requests.

Post-Fast Reflections

Use these pages to capture everything you experienced, felt, and heard from Yahweh throughout your 72 hours.

What did God reveal to you?

Continue your reflections...

Continue your reflections...

Continue your reflections...

www.ingramcontent.com/pod-product-compliance
Lightning Source LLC
Chambersburg PA
CBHW041649150726
48005CB00015BB/2565